EXPLORE AI

MACHINE LEARNING

SONYA NEWLAND

WAYLAND
www.waylandbooks.co.uk

First published in Great Britain in 2021 by Wayland

Copyright © Hodder & Stoughton Limited, 2021

 Produced for Wayland by
White-Thomson Publishing Ltd
www.wtpub.co.uk

All rights reserved.

Editor: Sonya Newland
Designer: Dan Prescott, Couper Street Type Co.

HB ISBN: 978 1 5263 1511 3
PB ISBN: 978 1 5263 1513 7
10 9 8 7 6 5 4 3 2 1

MIX
Paper from responsible sources
FSC® C104740
FSC www.fsc.org

Wayland
An imprint of Hachette Children's Group
Part of Hodder & Stoughton
Carmelite House
50 Victoria Embankment
London EC4Y 0DZ

An Hachette UK Company
www.hachette.co.uk
www.hachettechildrens.co.uk

Printed in Dubai

The publisher would like to thank the following for permission to reproduce their pictures:
Alamy: RGB Ventures/SuperStock 17m; Getty Images: Mark Ralston 19b; Shutterstock: Bluehousestudio 4t, 7tr, PureSolution 4b, vs148 5t, Willyam Bradberry 5m, sumkinn 5b, Maridav 6, katieromanoff_art 7tl, EQRoy 7b, Siberian Art 8t, Vectomart 8b, nullplus 9l, robuart 9r, pixelliebe 9r, VikaSuh 10 (all), Mangostar 11t, Patryk Kosmider 11mt, RoBird 11mb, Karramba Production 11b, Luis Molinero 12t, Andrew Rybalko 12b, Phonlamai Photo 13t, vladwel 13b, GraphicsRF.com 14t, Sailor Johnny 14m, GraphicsRF.com 14b, Nadia Snopek 15t, Alexander Oganezov 15b, Sammby 16l, Vitaly Art 16r, Anita Ponne 17t, MSSA 17b, Lightspring 18t, Eric Isselee 18mc, sebra 18ml, John Kasawa 18mr, Verisakeet 18br, FrimuFilms 19t, metamorworks 20t, NotionPic 20b, Sin314 21t, Andrew Krasovitckii 21b, Pavlo Plakhotia 22t, WAYHOME studio 22b, Sensvector 23t, graphic-line 24b, Blueastro 24–25, Martial Red 25b, MriMan 26t, Irina Strelnikova 26b, MONOPOLY919 27t, MonsieurSeb 27b, alekseiveprev 28, Phonlamai Photo 29t, agsandrew 29b.

All design elements from Shutterstock.

Every effort has been made to clear copyright. Should there be any inadvertent omission, please apply to the publisher for rectification.

The website addresses (URLs) included in this book were valid at the time of going to press. However, it is possible that contents or addresses may have changed since the publication of this book. No responsibility for any such changes can be accepted by either the author or the publisher.

You can find words in **bold** in the glossary on page 30.

CONTENTS

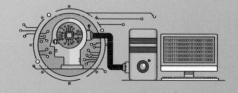

WHAT IS AI?

Artificial Intelligence (AI) is the science, technology and engineering of intelligent machines. AI is all around you – a part of your everyday life. A lot of the time you might not even realise that the devices you interact with are 'intelligent'!

AMAZING AI ABILITIES

The goal of AI is to create machines that use human-like intelligence to perform many different tasks. These might be practical jobs, such as mowing the lawn. But they may also be incredibly tricky tasks where the machine has to think and learn.

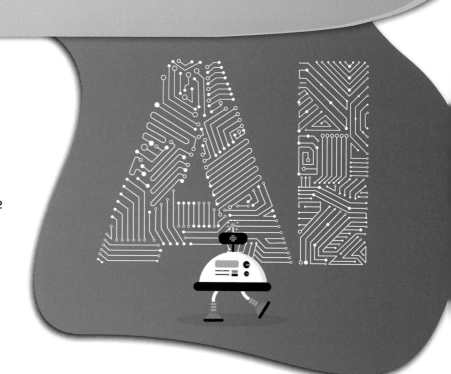

HUMANS – THE ULTIMATE MACHINES

Your brain is an amazing machine, carrying out complex processes every second of every day. It's how you think, feel, react, reason, analyse, learn and explain. Understanding human abilities like these is key to AI – recreating these processes in machines is what makes artificial intelligence so 'real'.

4

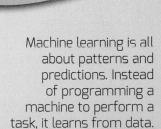

WHAT IS MACHINE LEARNING?

Machine learning is the basis for all AI. It gives systems, such as computers, robots and other devices, the ability to automatically learn and improve through experience, without being specifically programmed for a task. Machine learning works by interpreting **data** and making **predictions**. Think about it – the more you know about something, the better you understand it. It's the same with machine learning.

Machine learning is all about patterns and predictions. Instead of programming a machine to perform a task, it learns from data.

WHERE WILL IT LEAD?

As scientists and engineers work to build machines that learn more effectively and independently, some people have started to wonder whether this kind of learning is a good idea. Just because we *can* develop smarter machines with more human-like processes and abilities, does that mean we *should*? What if they become too clever or too human-like? What if we rely on them so much we start to lose skills ourselves? AI engineers consider **ethical** questions like these carefully in their work.

THINKING MACHINES

From the early days of computing, engineers wanted to create machines that did more than just respond to programmed instructions. They dreamed of building machines that could think and learn in a similar way to humans.

SMART OR DUMB?

Look at your computer, your phone, your fitness tracker... they probably all seem pretty smart, don't they? In fact, gadgets like these are often referred to as 'dumb' devices. They might be able to perform loads of different tasks, but they can only do so if we tell them what to do, and how. The secret to real smartness is giving computers the ability to think for themselves.

Devices such as smartphones and smart watches are examples of weak, or narrow, AI. Weak AI can get better at the job it was designed to do, but it can't learn new tasks.

WHAT'S THE PROBLEM?

People first began working on AI technology back in the 1940s. They realised pretty quickly that the ways in which computers could help humans were always going to be limited by humans' own knowledge. There were two key problems:

1. There are some things that even humans don't know how to do.

2. There are some things that we know how to do but that we can't explain clearly in a language that computers would understand – for example, riding a bike or driving a car.

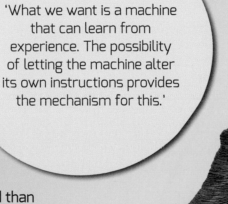

During the Second World War (1939–45), Alan Turing created a machine that cracked enemy codes. This is a sculpture of him studying the German Enigma machine.

TURING'S IDEA

'What we want is a machine that can learn from experience. The possibility of letting the machine alter its own instructions provides the mechanism for this.'

In 1947, brilliant British mathematician Alan Turing (1912–54) summed up the solution.

Creating such a device was easier said than done, of course, and Turing's 'learning machine' was never built. However, Turing was the first to suggest that a computer could learn by itself and become artificially intelligent.

BRIGHT MINDS

Arthur Samuel (1901–90) was an expert in the early days of artificial intelligence. He coined the term 'machine learning' in 1959, describing it as giving computers 'the ability to learn without being explicitly programmed'. Samuel went on to be a **pioneer** in computer gaming AI.

READ, GUESS, REFINE, REPEAT

For Turing and other early AI pioneers, a machine that could learn by itself was just a theory. Today, these machines are a reality – but what does 'learn by itself' really mean?

DEALING WITH DATA

It all starts with a whole load of data. A programmer gives the computer lots of examples of different questions and answers. The entire mass, or body, of this information is referred to as the **dataset**.

A question might be a picture of an object.

Q =

The answer might be the name of that object.

A = 'bus'

This teaches the computer about the *type* of information it might get.

Humans still have an important part to play in machine learning. We need to provide the examples that the computers use to learn from, and program computers to know how to identify when they're getting a guess wrong.

IT'S ALL GUESSWORK

Programmers give the computer examples of questions and answers, but they don't tell it how to find the right answer. In machine learning, the computer figures out a way to *guess* the right answer. It does this by looking for similar questions in the dataset that it has seen before.

WHAT IF...? Could we ever get to the point where machines are so good at teaching themselves that they no longer need humans to input the data they learn from? What if that happens? What advantages are there to making machines that are more intelligent than we are? What risks might there be?

At first, the computer's guesses – called predictions – are a bit random.

Then it starts comparing its guesses with what it knows are correct answers to similar questions in the dataset.

It uses these to reduce the mistakes it makes in its guesswork.

Slowly, it 'learns' from its mistakes, correcting itself as it goes along. Its predictions become more and more accurate.

DO YOU GET IT?

Your brain is an amazing machine. It can remember things you've learned before and apply **logic** and **reasoning** to predict what will happen, even in unfamiliar situations. As you've seen, machine learning works using a similar process.

MACHINE TALENT

At the moment, most artificial intelligence is based on processes that computers already do well. Think about the different subjects you study at school. Which one do you think a machine would be best at?

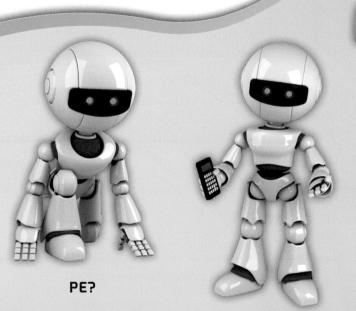

ART?

LITERATURE?

Since the first calculating machines were invented, computers have been better at maths than humans!

PE?

MATHS?

FINDING PATTERNS

Machines are also good at collecting and searching through masses of data to find key words and patterns. In fact, machines are brilliant at interpreting complex data. You can see this in many everyday examples of machine learning AI.

Facial recognition software is AI that recognises patterns in images to identify individuals in different photographs.

GPS (global positioning systems) send information to computers about the location of vehicles. The computers use patterns in this data to predict where and when traffic is likely to be busy on a regular basis.

Normal anti-**virus** software can only recognise viruses it has been programmed to identify. But machine learning is starting to help make predictions about new viruses based on coding patterns in existing ones.

READING YOUR MIND?

Type any letter you like into an internet search engine. What predictions does the engine come up with for what the rest of the word will be? As you use a particular search engine, over time you'll notice that it gets better at predicting what you're looking for by learning from your past searches. That's machine learning in action!

The search results you get when you type something into Google aren't created by a team of people! It would be impossible to **manually** categorise all the information on the World Wide Web. Google's machine learning whizzes through millions of pages and guesses which articles are relevant to your search.

AI
IN ACTION

UNDERSTANDING

HUMANS...

Humans have always asked questions – to solve practical problems and to try to find the answers to life's great mysteries! 'Cognition' is the word we use to describe how we gain knowledge and understanding. Humans have several key **cognitive** skills.

PERCEPTION: This means recognising and interpreting information from our senses.

ATTENTION: There are three types of attention:

• Sustained attention helps you to stay focused on one task for a long period of time.

• Selective attention helps you to stay focused despite distractions.

• Divided attention helps you to do two things at once.

MEMORY: There are two types of memory:

• Long-term memory stores and allows you to recall information you learned in the past.

• Short-term, or working, memory helps you to recall what you need to know for the task you are doing at a given moment.

LANGUAGE: We recognise sounds and understand them as words. We can also generate speech of our own.

FLEXIBILITY AND CONTROL: This allows us to change *what* we think about and *how* we think about it through experience.

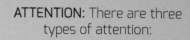

PROCESSING: We process information both visually and **spacially**, to recognise the relationship between objects.

Humans understand the world through practical processes, but we are also influenced by other 'inputs', such as emotions and opinions.

...VS. MACHINES

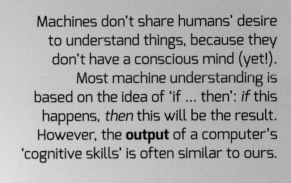

PATTERN RECOGNITION: Computers identify patterns in data to understand what that data means and use logic to predict what will happen next based on that pattern.

CATEGORY FORMATION: This is the ability to sort information into categories. It's key to being able to evaluate and analyse information.

PROCESSING: Like humans, machines may process information using 'visual' data, for example from cameras, and measurements to predict the relationship between objects.

Machines don't share humans' desire to understand things, because they don't have a conscious mind (yet!). Most machine understanding is based on the idea of 'if ... then': *if* this happens, *then* this will be the result. However, the **output** of a computer's 'cognitive skills' is often similar to ours.

MEMORY: Machines usually have two types of memory:

• Short-term memory stores information that is needed only while a process is running.

• Long-term memory stores data and files that can be retrieved at any time.

FLEXIBILITY AND CONTROL: Thanks to machine learning, AI computers can adapt what and how they 'think' based on previous experience.

Machines don't have sentiment – emotions or opinions. Their understanding of the world is based on data and logic.

EXPLORING ALGORITHMS

One of a computer's key 'cognitive skills' is pattern recognition. Part of this is identifying logical steps and sequences. We all follow rules and processes to help us get things done, and computers are no different. They are programmed to follow steps to achieve a task.

AMAZING ALGORITHMS

The steps a machine follows are called **algorithms**. An algorithm is basically a set of instructions for completing a task successfully. You could think of an algorithm as a computer's thought process.

An algorithm for making toast might be:

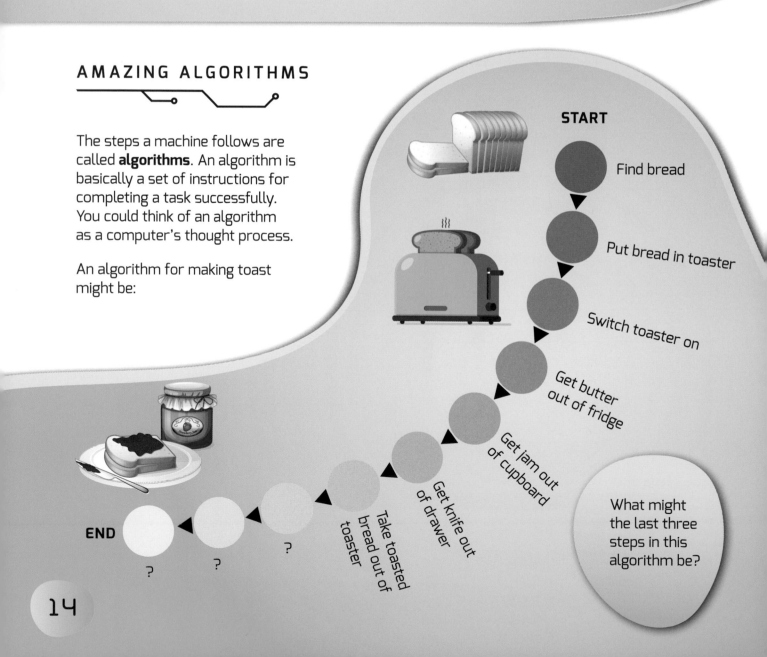

START

Find bread

Put bread in toaster

Switch toaster on

Get butter out of fridge

Get jam out of cupboard

Get knife out of drawer

Take toasted bread out of toaster

?

?

?

END

What might the last three steps in this algorithm be?

14

The first algorithm we know about dates from the ancient Babylonian culture, in 1600 BCE. This series of calculations was carved into clay tablets. They not only solve specific problems, but also contain general solutions to different groups, or classes, of problem.

BRUTE FORCE

A brute force algorithm is used to solve problems. It searches everywhere in a dataset, but it doesn't look for short-cuts to find the information it needs. It's a bit like a game of hide-and-seek, where the seeker's strategy is simply to look everywhere – upstairs and down, indoors and out – even in places where a hider wouldn't fit! If there's a solution, brute force will find it... eventually. But it's not very efficient.

TRAINING ALGORITHMS

Ordinary computers use algorithms all the time, and artificial intelligence uses some algorithms based on brute force. So, what's different about real 'machine learning' algorithms? Machine learning is about *training* algorithms so that they make decisions on their own.

The Nest Learning Thermostat is a wi-fi-controlled smart thermostat that helps users to save energy. The secret to the science lies in its machine learning algorithm. For a week, users manually control the thermostat. The algorithm uses this dataset to learn what temperatures people want and when. It knows when no one is home and automatically switches to energy-saving mode!

AI
IN ACTION

SOLVING PROBLEMS

Machine learning, and the special type of machine learning called deep learning (see pages 18–19), both work using algorithms. In basic machine learning, algorithms interpret and learn from data, then use it to make a prediction to perform the task at hand.

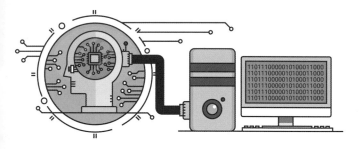

SUPERVISED LEARNING

AI engineers divide machine learning into the different types of problem it can tackle. Supervised learning deals with problems where data exists that can be used to train the algorithm. The algorithm improves by recognising and responding to feedback. Identifying objects is an example of supervised learning. If the computer guesses wrong, it learns from this feedback and makes an improved guess next time.

PROBLEMS, PROBLEMS...

Machines learn in different ways in supervised learning.

Classification problems are where a machine is given a set of information and learns to classify, or identify, them.

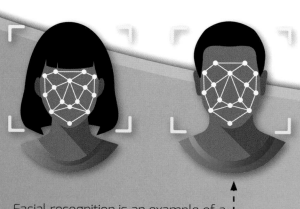

Facial recognition is an example of a classification problem.

UNDERSTANDING NEURONS

Some machine learning uses a set of algorithms that are made up of lots of interconnected **neurons**. In AI, a neuron is an element that receives and processes data. The different 'layers' of algorithms mean that the machine learns more effectively because of the detail it can identify.

Artificial neural networks (see page 21) were inspired by the way that information is transmitted and processed by the human brain.

The clever thing about neurons in machine learning is that they can draw on **input** data from *any* previous event. This makes it much more likely that the prediction (the output) will be correct.

BRIGHT MINDS

Marvin Minsky (1927–2016) was an American cognitive and computer scientist. In 1951, Minsky created the first artificial neural network, which was very influential in AI. Minsky later established the AI laboratory at the famous Massachusetts Institute of Technology (MIT) in the USA.

Reinforcement learning problems are when a program interacts with a particular environment and makes decisions along the way. It learns and improves from past mistakes.

Games such as chess are an examples of reinforcement problems.

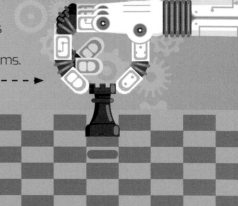

HOW DO YOU KNOW?

Deep learning is a type of machine learning that uses neural networks. In deep learning, data is processed in 'layers', which allows machines to fully understand and solve problems.

YOUR BRILLIANT BRAIN

In the human brain, any neuron can connect to any other neuron. Each connection performs a separate task. This creates a huge, complex network that allows our brains to function in an incredibly advanced way.

DELVING DEEPER

Deep learning uses a 'deep' or 'large' neural network. This is arranged in layers, which work in specific ways and directions. The first layer takes the input data, does a particular task, then passes the data on to the second layer. That layer performs its own task and sends the result on to the third layer, and so on.

The difference between human and machine neural networks can be seen in the way we **deduce** things.

If we learn that a lion is dangerous, our brain will deduce that a crocodile is also dangerous.

Deep learning can classify a lion as dangerous, but it won't automatically deduce that a crocodile is also dangerous based on that knowledge.

LAYERS AND WEBS

Deep learning happens in layers, while the connections that allow human learning are more like a web. However, the processes are quite similar. Each layer, or level, in an artificial neural network provides a different interpretation of the data. Your brain processes problems by applying different concepts and related questions to the problem.

CODE-CRACKING

Deep learning may be the answer to cracking even the most complex codes, because it can make sense of things in a multi-stage process in the blink of an eye. It might even be able to do that better than the brain's neural web can. And your brain is already pretty smart...

1 B37 YOU C4N R34D 7H15 W17H0U7 3V3N 7H1NK1NG 4B0U7 17!

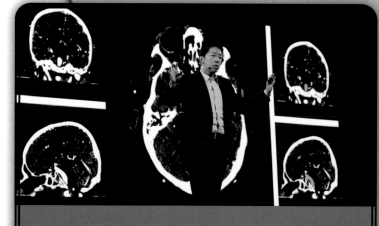

BRIGHT MINDS

Andrew Ng (b. 1976) is an American computer scientist. He founded Google Brain – a special team at Google that works on deep learning AI. Google Brain has created deep learning that improves images, translates languages and increases online security. Ng has also used deep learning in online education to help students all over the world.

NEURAL NETWORKS

HUMANS...

The human brain and the nervous system work together to process information. The nervous system is a network of nerves that send messages between the brain and different parts of the body.

1. The nervous system takes in information through the senses.

2. It sends the information to the brain via neurons, or nerve cells.

The brain stem links the spinal cord to the brain.

The spinal cord runs from your brain down your back. Nerves reach out from the spinal cord to all your organs and other body parts.

3. The brain processes the information and sends messages back to the body on how to react.

The brain and nervous system control everything about us – our emotions, our behaviour and even our dreams!

...VS. MACHINES

1. Input data goes into the first layer of neurons – the input layer.

2. Data is processed through a series of hidden layers.

In machines, a neural network functions in a similar way. The central computer processor is like the brain. Input data is like the information you receive from the outside world, sent to the brain for processing via layers of neurons.

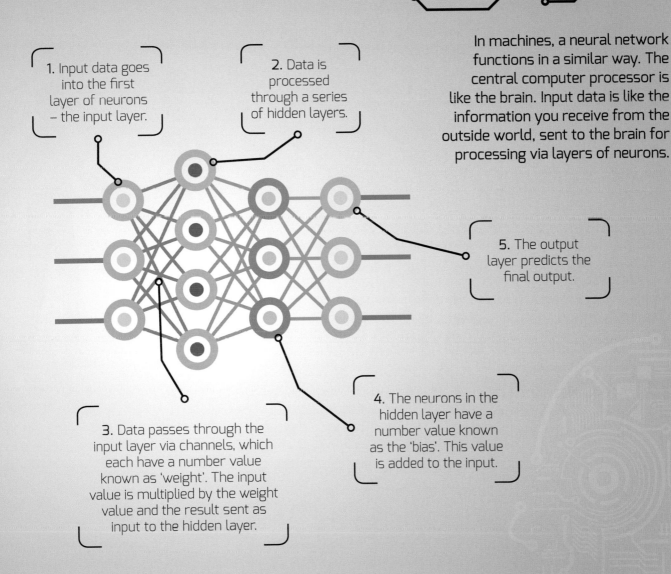

5. The output layer predicts the final output.

4. The neurons in the hidden layer have a number value known as the 'bias'. This value is added to the input.

3. Data passes through the input layer via channels, which each have a number value known as 'weight'. The input value is multiplied by the weight value and the result sent as input to the hidden layer.

In AI, neural networks control a machine's output data – its responses and predictions.

WHAT'S YOUR RESPONSE?

Humans use **common sense**, logic and what they've learned from experience to react and respond to the world around them. Machine learning is allowing AI technology to react to the world in a similar way.

REINFORCEMENT LEARNING

You saw on page 17 how one form of machine learning is 'reinforcement learning'. This means that computers can interpret and respond to different factors in their environment. These might be physical objects that a machine avoids or interacts with, or it might be responding to human interaction. Reinforcement learning is the force behind an important area of AI technology...

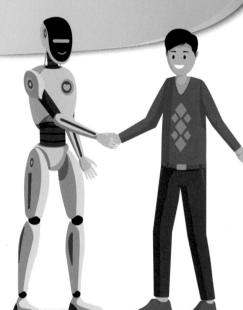

Machine learning uses patterns in data to identify what kind of music you like.

GETTING TO KNOW YOU

When you download a song, you get recommendations of other songs you might like. When you watch a video, you'll see an 'Up next' list jam-packed with other videos the machine predicts you might enjoy. Machine learning algorithms have figured out what you like, searched their dataset, and responded with suggestions for what you should listen to or watch next.

SELF-DRIVING CARS

Smart cars are another key example of machine learning in action. Engineers are creating AI algorithms that could create vehicles that are fully **autonomous**.

Machine learning then allows it to identify an object and decide how to react to it.

Computer vision technology allows the car to 'see' objects.

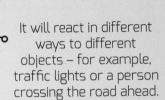

It will react in different ways to different objects – for example, traffic lights or a person crossing the road ahead.

AI IN ACTION

Waymo is a US company that is busy creating technology to put self-driving cars on the road. In 2017, it launched Waymo One, a self-driving taxi service. Users call a Waymo One using an **app** on their phone – like a taxi, but without the driver! In 2020, Waymo Via started using driverless trucks for transporting goods.

WHAT IF...? Some people say that driverless cars would be too dangerous on our roads. Others argue that this is only because they are filled with human-driven cars, and humans are not always safe drivers! What if there were *only* driverless cars on the roads? Would that make it safer?

REACTIONS

HUMANS...

One of our amazing cognitive skills (see pages 12–13) is the ability to react to our environment. This involves, detecting, processing and responding to things we **perceive** through our senses. One of the most important things our reactions do is keep us safe!

2. The information travels via the nervous system to the brain.

1. We see, hear, feel, smell or taste something in the world around us.

3. Our brain filters out the unimportant information.

4. It interprets the important information.

5. It sends messages to other parts of our body in the form of reactions, such as stopping on the kerb if we see a car coming, or spitting out food if it has gone bad before it makes us sick!

In humans, the time it takes to spot a danger and apply the brakes is between 0.7 and 3 seconds.

...VS. MACHINES

1. The car 'sees' an object by an image recognition system (traffic lights, pedestrians, street signs, lines on the road, etc.).

2. Neural networks identify patterns in the data.

Intelligent machines also perceive their environment and take action. The purpose of their reactions is to maximise their chances of success at a task. They use simulations of human senses to do this. Image recognition systems work together with machine learning to allow machines such as self-driving cars to react safely.

3. They feed this information to machine-learning algorithms.

4. The algorithms interpret the data and send messages back to the software that cause it to react in certain ways – for example, to drive within the lines, slow down because the light is turning amber or pull over because an emergency vehicle is coming up behind.

In an autonomous car, braking reaction time is about 0.5 seconds.

MACHINE LEARNING AND MEDICINE

Machine learning is being used to make our lives easier and better in many different ways. But one of the most important areas where AI and machine learning could really change our lives for the better is in medicine.

DIAGNOSING DISEASES

Often there aren't enough specialist doctors to see and **diagnose** all the patients that have a particular disease or problem.

Doctors diagnose diseases by recognising patterns, such as a pattern of particular symptoms. Machines are very good at identifying patterns, too – intelligent machines can even learn from these patterns. Deep learning algorithms are now able to learn from data to correctly diagnose diseases quickly.

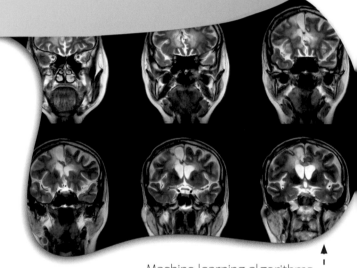

Machine learning algorithms can look at medical images, such as brain scans, and identify complications very accurately.

A PERSONAL PLAN

Robots are already used to help perform surgeries. Some AI-powered robots can use data from previous surgeries to improve or even create new techniques.

But it doesn't stop there. Once a disease has been diagnosed, AI may be able to work out the best treatment plan for a particular patient. Everyone responds to drugs and treatment schedules differently. Machine learning can predict a patient's likely response depending on different factors.

DRUG DEVELOPMENT

Machine learning is also used in the development of medicines. Usually it takes years of trial and error to develop drugs for particular diseases. It is also very expensive. But drug development involves a lot of evaluation and analysis – the perfect job for machine learning to help cut time and costs.

WHAT IF...? What if we come to rely almost completely on artificial intelligence to diagnose diseases? Machine learning isn't perfect – it doesn't always make the correct predictions. So what happens when it makes a mistake? Is our health an area we want to trust to algorithms? But human doctors make mistakes too, so are we actually safer in the hands of computers?

THE FUTURE OF MACHINE LEARNING

Machine learning is the basis of all AI – which means that it holds the secrets to future AI tech. So what are AI experts working on now, and where might AI be in a few years' time?

WHAT DO WE WANT AND WHAT CAN WE DO?

Developments in machine learning will probably take us down two paths – in two different directions.

In some ways, the direction machine learning will take may depend on what ideas people have for AI technology – what do they want it to achieve? What intelligent gadget would *you* like to see developed?

In other ways, as experts work to improve machine learning and deep learning algorithms, they might discover things that it can do that no one has even thought of yet!

INTELLIGENT ARTIFICIAL FRIENDS

Conversational AI is technology that allows humans and machines to talk to and interact with each other. It's what makes chatbots and virtual personal assistants, such as Amazon's Alexa, work. Experts are developing machine learning that will improve these interactions.

Machine learning may soon power robots with completely human-like minds and abilities.

WHOLE-BRAIN EMULATION

Whole-brain **emulation** is as complicated – and amazing – as it sounds! Also known as 'mind upload', this is a way of scanning the human brain, or the neural codes in it, and uploading them to a computer. That way, what's stored in your brain can be kept forever.

At the moment, whole-brain emulation is just a theory – there's no way of doing it – but how long will it be before technology like this is a reality?

WHAT IF...? In whole-brain emulation, our brain function could be stored, then retrieved by someone else after we have died. Some people feel that this is a way of cheating death. What if scientists really do achieve whole-brain emulation one day? Is it morally right to use AI to make ourselves 'immortal' in this way? Should we focus on developing AI for more worthy purposes? How might the human race benefit from having access to some people's brilliant brains?

GLOSSARY

algorithm – a set of steps that tell a computer what to do in order to solve a problem or perform a task

app – an application designed for a mobile device, such as a smartphone

autonomous – describes things that have the power to make their own decisions

cognitive – describes things relating to the process of gaining knowledge and understanding

common sense – good judgement in practical matters

data – information such as facts and statistics that are collected and analysed

dataset – a collection of related sets of information that a computer can interpret and manipulate

deduce – to work something out by logical reasoning

diagnose – to identify a type of problem or illness

ethical – relating to whether things are right or wrong

emulation – when something's function or behaviour is copied or reproduced

facial recognition – software that can map out facial features in order to identify individuals in images

GPS – global positioning system, a system that allows people to navigate using information sent and received by satellites orbiting Earth

input – information or data that is put into a machine or computer

logic – a way of thinking about something based on sensible reasoning

manually – by hand rather than using a machine

neuron – a nerve cell that carries messages around the body and to the brain in the form of electrical impulses

output – the information that comes out of a computer after it has been processed

perceive – to make a judgement based on seeing and understanding something

pioneer – someone who is the first to explore, develop or use a particular idea or thing

prediction – a guess that an intelligent machine makes at what is the correct answer to a question or problem

reasoning – working through information logically to reach the right answer

software – the programs that give computers the instructions they need to work

spacially – in a way that relates to space and the position of objects within an area

virus – a piece of computer code that can copy itself and steal or destroy data on a computer

FIND OUT MORE

BOOKS

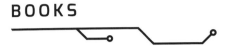

AI (The Tech Head Guide) by William Potter (Wayland, 2020)

Computers (The Tech Head Guide) by William Potter (Wayland, 2020)

WEBSITES

www.bbc.co.uk/teach/alan-turing-creator-of-modern-computing/zhwp7nb

Find out all about computer genius Alan Turing.

www.bbc.co.uk/newsround/49274918

Discover more about what AI is and what it does.

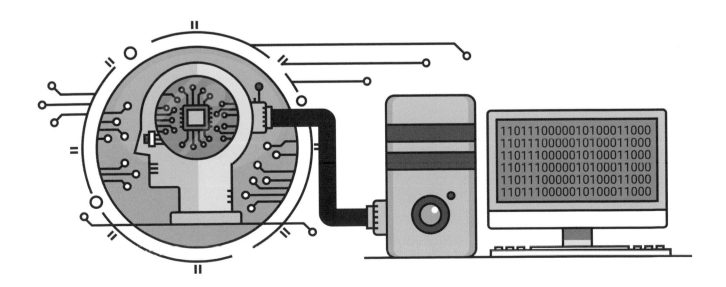

INDEX